In *Omitting All That is Usually Said*, Robin Caton, re-creates the anatomy of perception, with its "folly of love" as language, narrating passages of consciousness where "light is a gaze" that opens out into a world of metaphoric rhythms. Through a series of dynamic interactions, torn detours and sequences, and "lateral fictions" between an omniscient observer, a protagonist on a train, and windows that carry the "intimate air" of landscapes, Caton demonstrates a painter's ability to create a "lucid invention" you'll want to read again and again. Imagine a story, en media res, full of subtext and vision play—archives of indefinite time made for our "starved minds" like "insects…in stuttering debate." This magical collection invites Mallarmé's declaration that "Every soul is a melody to be renewed."

—Elena Karina Byrne, author of *If This Makes You Nervous*

Robin Caton's *Omitting All That Is Usually Said* floats in space and time, through thought and action, leaving in its wake so many beautifully structured turns toward what is unavailable to most of us, so much of perception and consciousness, which is to say, most of life itself. That this omission becomes so embodied in this work is its engagement with the awe of presence, of being. An exploratory lyric runs up against a traditional narrative of a lonely man on a train seeking love and connection, landscape becomes lyric, story becomes spirit, and book becomes originary, once again a place where we can experience the difficulty, even the beauty, of becoming.

—Gillian Conoley, author of *Notes from the Passenger*

In this "womb of words," Robin Caton gives the reader the just born joy of the day, along with its quotidian continuity. The sadness of failed but persistent love is an underlying refrain. There is a musicality in Caton's words as she questions consciousness ("I am the name for things") and being ("We walk in/ the wind through everyday/ terms, matter as sound . . .."). Narratives appear and disappear in the juxtaposed poetry and prose, and in the broken words of collages that serve as a visual counterpoint to the text. An eternal, but always ending, spring is invoked. This "linguistic paradise" presents the beauty of the world in all its poignant transitory glory. *Omitting All That is Usually Said* does just that, while somehow managing to say everything.

—Laura Moriarty, author of *Personal Volcano*

Also by Robin Caton

The Color of Dusk (Omnidawn, 2001)

Omitting All That is Usually Said

Cover art by Afsaneh Michaels
cover art title: Nothing to Hold Onto

Cover design by Robin Caton and Laura Joakimson
Interior design by Laura Joakimson
Cover typeface: Komet
Interior typeface: Century Gothic and Adobe Garamond

Library of Congress Cataloging-in-Publication Data

Names: Caton, Robin, author.
Title: Omitting all that is usually said / Robin Caton.
Description: Oakland, California : Omnidawn Publishing, 2024. | Summary:
"In Omitting All That is Usually Said, Robin Caton explores the nature
of light, form, language, meaning, and thought, alongside the complexity
of their interwoven relationships. Caton interrogates the workings of
the human mind and explores the way we integrate disparate perceptions.
Caton questions whether we can be certain that things really exist and
that all we experience isn't simply a play of light and shadow. She
considers how we live with all the limitations and emotional turmoil
imbedded in humanity, while also maintaining a sense of something we
call perfection. The poems of Omitting All That is Usually Said
investigate how we might capture the depths of conflicting experiences
and lived knowledge in ways that we can comprehend, and they marvel at
how we find delight in all of it"-- Provided by publisher.

Identifiers: LCCN 2024013047 | ISBN 9781632431554 (trade paperback)
Subjects: LCGFT: Poetry.
Classification: LCC PS3553.A855 O45 2024 | DDC 811/.54--dc23/eng/20240325
LC record available at https://lccn.loc.gov/2024013047

Published by Omnidawn Publishing, Oakland, California
www.omnidawn.com
10 9 8 7 6 5 4 3 2 1
ISBN: 978-1-63243-155-4

Omitting All That is Usually Said

Robin Caton

OMNIDAWN PUBLISHING
OAKLAND, CALIFORNIA
2024

CONTENTS

I'd like to talk about the perfection underlying life
when the mind is covered over with perfection
and the heart is filled with delight
but I wish not to deny the rest.
In our minds, there is awareness of perfection;
when we look with our eyes we see it,
and how it functions is mysterious to us and unavailable.
—Agnes Martin, *Writings*

IN TIME

The deep booming note of a huge Buddhist temple bell resounded at leisurely intervals, and the lingering reverberations held an awareness of the old Japan and of the flow of time. —Yasunari Kawabata, *Beauty and Sadness*

He tried, the first time brief, a few things in the dawn
of the world present at those distant locations.

Look, my dear, you were his sky. It was not a blind bordering.
Even art became a unique light signature, feathery detail,
a world of promise for the bird that it contained.

It is also a place of bending, green, violet,
the morning you inhabit, the use of words,
light named before you were living,
an arrangement of landscape after you observe
and then perhaps to confuse.

Slowly: move your head. Tree, crying, manifests rain,
a special conjunction of non-gray and white.

ender bo_
ring from its n cu_

               wax
: this be memory
              d forward
                oread like clou
                 inarticulable

WHITE ⁼LE

Twelve windows, grimed with dirt, ran along the length of the other side of the car of the Amtrak express. Robert noticed that the one on the far end was open. He could not stop staring at it.

The windows on his side of the car were sealed shut. He was one of only a few passengers in the car. Leaning against the wall, his briefcase on his lap, he watched the open window. It would not keep to a consistent pattern: sometimes it slid down slowly, sometimes it jiggled and slid more quickly, sometimes it seemed to stop, take a breath, and remain where it was.

To watch that window sliding toward its ultimate state—complete openness—alarmed him. He began thinking about the past.

Why do I feel this naïve consciousness break,
splinter into presence while we talk yet again
of whitish-green blossoms, wind, the new dead
above the silvery branches, staked through the
heart with numbness?

We see neither tree nor water. We, who have
touched the roughness, a trace of the artist's
complex breeze, frighten in the cold blood
of green familiar country, and in such common
colors, turn the plum yellow while we speak
of the uncaring grass touched by silken light.

Do not believe the first, cold objects,
the murderous threads of colored glass.
Such things and such atoms tell what has
happened but do not believe it. Physics may
say an evening shower passed but the waves,
the blackness, hover as hill overhead.

We, who speak, have the same dark thought.
We see, we hear, willing to be ruined.
The quivering world creaks on, depending on us.

It was the fifth of April. Robert was going to New York for a meeting. For how many years had he been making these trips? When did the Amtrak express from Philadelphia to New York begin? Probably he'd gone at least six times a year ever since. Perhaps more.

How often had he watched the same houses, trees, and cars outside the train windows? Or past midnight, after a long meeting and the inevitable dinner that followed, caught a glimpse, on the way home, of a shimmering moon?

During these trips, which he always made without his wife, the boundary between city and suburb, county and state, soon disappeared. Borders were crossed before he could see the signs that marked them. The speed with which they traveled ensured that the scenery blurred, the space between stations a continuous flow that merged with the flow of time.

Light, shorn of the poem,
appears nowhere in the
ancient lexicon. Silent waves
of alternating air, the act of
viewing arrays itself through
idiom. A scene soon repeated,
the alphabet known as time
is found. For what other script
is natural? Consider its nature:
God, in a low-pitched lover's voice.

But later, under the stars, what then?
the more deeply, untellable stars?
—Rainer Maria Rilke, "Ninth Elegy"

But later, under the stars, we are faced
with particular beings, the bodies of
which there is no such thing as. This
imperfection is not merely composite.
In a true cosmos, such *no* implies weight.
Ensouled earth, secret slopes, the means
by which thick lines, hollows and bones,
attach to air. These objects, stirred
by human passion, present themselves
as unwitting wanderers. The double
spiral of subject must see what to do
in the mind's eye. Untellable stars
speak of light however we label form.

vision plays
waits. There
You are two
cage. Will y_{s: for-}
as quickly _{g the}
come for. T_{vernance}
Skepticism_{a wonder.}
You are m_{o room}
but you fe_{Foreign}
the huma_{e city's slopes.}
of terror._{, in jail!}
          .ows past.

~ncopated time and simply:
no fevered praise.
r sure who is in the
loubt you can move
ι are the one it has
nues at a slow pace.
ds contain this.
imb side-show way,
ıking, touching, all
ı wonder at your lack

ANG

Humid breeze, apparent patterns
buried earth far above the center.
Enclosed by shadow, quiet clouds,
worn as ideology. Sailing against
this immensity, a white bird soars.
I steer clear of wings. In twilight,
to see the stones made strangely
immaterial leads to uncertainty.
In my heart, heavy with visions,
I am the name for things.

IN LIGHT

When I say 'darkness,' I mean a privation of knowing, just as whatever you do not know or have forgotten is dark to you, because you do not see it with your spiritual eyes. —Anonymous, *The Cloud of Unknowing*

Tree beside a river. Fire, as Kant's water
touching wood. Such sweet eloquence
burning up, the prompt cause, and later
the destruction. To add more rapture,

might one first cut off the sun?
We infer from green the component grass
arranged with damp and bottomless earth.
Neither holy harp nor things perceived

say what we actually see. Try to paint it.
It certainly seems this risen roof is somehow
overgrown with praise. And then?
Eden's happy plains, a paradise sprung

from adoring lips, dewy each morning
in lowly white, lovely to the sight but
enough to make one contrary, clear light
roaming at the edge of unity, geometry

of heavens tunable in prose or verse,
experimental, impossible to look at,
wide waving landscape, wood facing fire,
situated as object even if space is curved.

After the outskirts of Philadelphia came the towns and roads of New Jersey. At the journey's end there was the long, dark tunnel under the Hudson into New York.

There were so many trains entering and leaving Penn Station at once that the screech of brakes, the clanging of rails, the recorded voices announcing arrivals and departures mingled into a single roar that left little room for the small, familiar sound of Robert's own thoughts.

A star now repeated the six-edged
evolution inscribed by resinous earth
as though in violet silk. Scooped from
the perfection of memory, the sun

caused bluish light to appear in the
heart of day. Evening, wandering alone
through the smell of tar and tea, suggested
fullness of spirit, inwardly becoming

the reddish rings of unimpeded will.
And why? The brain rests on wind.
Selective cloud, containing within itself
mercy, a new erratic and eye-less nature

that the darkening air will re-draw.
Something of the grave retreated near
the uncanny origin of diffraction. To know
the star-hard feat called *departing*, by which

shadow imagines obscuring the wandering sea,
we must have woven moonlight where none
should be. What odd symmetrical genius rests
on the art of denial performed by light—

Matter revolutioni___ ...he way there
sense. The explos e gate-keepers —
I, caught, retreats nocents. Bloodless.
of the weather. W
telephones are fal
And then. So. Wl th, multiple cells
ontology of this i shing continuously
pajamas when su formulaically.
Check the date. l .: *The tangerine*
the angel, flutters
are dry. On some *ips to reveal the pearly*
page angels. On *tired windpipes heave*
phanous blue pills
ngine in the thick storm.

quick regard of
t in its particulars.
1. Mellifluousness
line? These
y sense of talking.
age holes. The
wn echoed
a thought!
ng, then time,
oks? My wings
listling. On this
ng.

not as angle/line/
irve/curve/curve
back on itself like

rune.it. The in/

hed. Ir
le

The other passengers would stand, take down their suitcases or backpacks from the racks above, put on their coats and hold their cell phones to their ears. Robert would stay seated, letting the others go first. As the sights and sounds of arrival swirled around him, he would think back over the weeks or months since he'd made this trip last. He always found it surprising.

Sometimes his feelings were sad or regretful. Sometimes he was excited and filled with anticipation. Even when the people around him were particularly rude or loud, the feeling of being back again in New York echoed within his body.

For a long time, he had wanted to stay in the city for more than a single day. That had been his thought again this week, and he had impulsively booked two nights at a luxury hotel. He would explore. Perhaps he would get symphony tickets or go to a museum.

He had also been influenced by the deep wish to see Alys again, to have dinner together, or take her to a play. They had not been in contact since she'd move to New York, but he knew she had a gallery show this week. As far as he knew, she was unattached.

a greyish bird
the size perhaps of two
plump sparrows
fallen in some field
—Denise Levertov,
The Mockingbird of
Mockingbirds

Here is a thing before question, a place of
walls, rooms of soul, where darkness is not
made of instants but of bells. White-gold eyes
shadow into greyish sea, a lucid invention.

Little to go on. And no one knows its own kind,
with birds, with bells. Just the life of the present
thinking, emptying, suggesting *fallen in a field*.
Two plump sparrows and neither begins.

The incessant one is turning simple, is such
ceremony soon swimming with birds.
Suggesting the lord of a thousand rival
nightingales, the size, perhaps, of bells.

All objects stop your thinking. You have reached
a conclusion. It may be defective. Plump birds
in a dim light purify the sky that lends assistance,
white-gold song, a thousand fields as presence.

49 W   *f questions,*
                         ɔrd or a sentence,

63 BL   ᴏʟ ꜱMOND JABÈS

        ·reproac'

71 BLɪnder).

    72 *in th'*

    74 he f'

    75 ˈeˑˑied.

    76 _

    78 ˈod's word emulating silence. If we

    80 ꞉l uth, too, explodes: invent phrases.

        ꞉ *f I sang? Running my face through*

            gs, in-breath, pause. Refrain,
            l, this God of yours?

            the flock. The
            h half crackeɾ

                he page. *I ·*

Robert had arrived at the Thirtieth Street Station early this morning. At this time of life, he disliked making reservations; the pressure to catch a particular train caused him to rush through his early routine. Instead, he preferred to move slowly and leave home when he was ready.

On weekdays, the early morning trains were often full, but today was Saturday and he'd had no trouble buying a ticket. He found the train convenient—much more so than driving, especially if he planned to return late. There were many trains throughout the day, some faster and some slower. He liked having the choice. He always made his trips to New York by train. Some people commuted daily and he knew them by sight.

Once aboard, Robert was surprised to find how few passengers there were. Perhaps there never were many people on the first Saturday express. It might be crowded later.

As he kept watching the window slide down, he began to think of fate.

The morning bell, symptomatic of rain,
crocodiles recurring in starved minds,
actual flowers and a pale green frame.
So logical, so lasting, otherwise he would
not believe it. A dog barks. The wavering
wind is one of the finest answers. Floating
in crystal, object of fire and shadow, he
reads that the soul spends a thousand nights
in the garden. Birds, which once had choice,
meet by chance, south of the river, doubters
planting a row of crosses and stars. Insects
seek to record each other in stuttering debate
and pay no heed to the moon. Looking up,
some feel only despair. Illogical, unreal,
nothing to name. His sole fear is the bell.

Swift clouds, loose rains,
toward a strictly pictorial
field. We walk in
the wind through everyday
terms, matter as sound
veering toward sky, ice-age
words predictably wet in
the blinding glare. And
in all the windows,
should we wish to
look, the red wave
breaks in flight. Azure
dawns, our special city,
the thoughts we need
to distinguish form, they
will be blinding, they
will be listening, perhaps
of sunlight. *Hurry*, we
speculate, *learn the associative
links*. Yet in all
the windows lit by
brightness and sky, no
object, no final meaning
to be carried there.

IN MIND

Here are some questions any of us might ask about ourselves: What am I? What is consciousness? Could I survive my bodily death? —Simon Blackburn, *Think*

It is not you who chooses to awaken.
Light is a gaze, formless, without object.

Ocean merging with empty beach, light, brightness,
breaks down time in which redemption, perishing

in golden fire, alters ordinary sweetness.
It is not elemental, this sudden field of *notice*.

The self is seen, seized—a release of light in human
opposition that celebrates itself through passion.

That great cosmic being known as Night Sky enchains
its throne to Eros. Glimpsed, light is dawn,

the sun in clay. Angels, planets, stars never dream.
And you? You are a painting, altered by sound.

The ancient, eyeless sun gods donned simple vestments
to leave this life, edging along their crimson halls

from room to smaller room. It is not you who
chooses. Light is not the absence of your name.

Just then the conductor came through to punch his ticket. "Where is everyone today?" Robert asked.

"Still sleeping. Bunch of lazy bones."

"Will it be full later?"

"No, it usually isn't. Not on a Saturday at this time of year."

After the conductor left, Robert looked around the car and saw two backpacks on the rack over what seemed to be empty seats. One was black and one green. They had stickers and markings all over them. The owners must be young. Probably they were in the small outdoor area between the cars, smoking.

How can language appear to itself as other than itself, so that it can interrogate and reflect upon itself?

Or must we be forever relegated to the already said or sayable, the already known?

Empire. Country under rule.

Purple. Certain serious aspects of the pending storm. *In lamplight, how the purple whirls.*

and if it's god
you're listening for?

   wedged forward
   letters spread like cloud
   grammar inarticulable
 onder
PURPLE

Houses flew by in a blur outside the windows. Far above the roofs, heavy gray clouds darkened the sky, seemingly about to empty rain over the earth.

But as the train went on, the sky cleared. Weak sunlight slanting in the windows reached Robert's side of the car. As they passed an industrial park, he could see the ground was dotted with puddles. On the other side a few spindly birch trees were just beginning to bud.

I survey the intimate air, vulgar light
imported for every demonstrable memory,

a womb of words merely the deceptive ability
to admit in nine nights the invention of light,

transparent, white, a *thing* that must
possess a mode of understanding so lost

it cannot appear but cloaks yellow air.
Moon in the folds, thought a verbal formula,

I walk. I see sweet arguments breathe.
Theology, imagination, emotional excitement

as they really are—blue cloud, a certain mode
of consciousness, consciousness itself transparent

gold, daughter of heaven in a flimsy dress,
locked in deception, spirit demonstrable,

a thing plain, right there, impossible to know,
which becomes the mother of reading.

I have written *daylilies, white* not to explain but to
pay attention. Something else has in mind the spring.

The teenagers who owned the backpacks returned from wherever they'd been. As soon as they sat, they took out their phones. They photographed each other making various faces—a grin, a snarl, a self-satisfied smirk. By the time the train drew near to the place where it entered the underground tunnel, they grew bored and closed their eyes. They seemed to fall asleep immediately.

The early spring day was only just beginning. Robert let his eyes follow a line of cars waiting at a stoplight, and then looked up into the now clear sky. For several moments thin rays of sunlight touched his face through the open window on the other side of the car. But suddenly the train entered the tunnel, and all became dark.

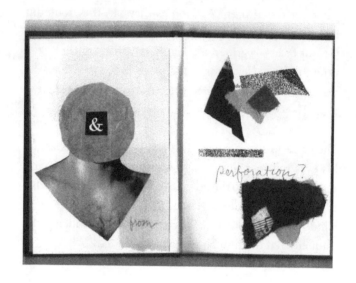

and they will reproach us
with those eyes...
asking why we
allowed this
—Lucille Clifton, the last day

This stab, this uncommon signature
in a language half-blind about truth,
as light suffers itself to encounter
constant air, arbiter of night soaked
yellowish-blue, a revolutionary love
too deep to tender embassy, to see,
for example, these feeble eyes, their
nature beguiled by fashionable words
of fracture, wild voices domesticated
by field theory, rare plain heart touched
by another complex encounter, asking
why we suffer it to happen. Voices able
to say: *this simple green*, being our life,
swift motion, and to us, for example,
blue, intermediary between blue and
yellow, somewhat greenish, a present-
absent color like a word, erotically real,
slinking down to a slight purging sound
able to reproach, asking why we allow it,
why we abide with two eyes alone.

SPATIAL CONCEPT

From the outset I never called the work I was doing ... painting, I called it a "spatial concept." This is because for me painting is a matter of ideas... The things I am doing at the moment are just variations on my two fundamental ideas: the hole and the cut.

—Lucio Fontana, Interview, 1967

For he was in a high fever and when he had
for a long time lain unconscious in a deathly
sweat so that his life was despaired of, he
was baptized. —Saint Augustine, *Confessions*

To compare many signs, songs awakened inquiry,
precious sentences, tranquil and of night.

That your life was despaired of.
It happened twice.

A tender cry of costuming white, your pauperized
spirit forgetting its richer nature.

It rained that night. The curtains formed a forgetting,
empire of yellow gesture under scarlet gaze.

If one wrote *abandonment* it provoked revolt.
You confessed you would rather not.

For a high fever nursed was a cry for help.
Who could stare at the sun?

Time had stayed unconscious, delicate lilac,
a Roman monarch to ruin a radiant morning.

And when you had for so long lain, forgetting
your wish for a light, untroubled life,

a delicate wind drew lines in pitch dark,
white-white, like a crow the snow reformed.

er body, t

from its

s be memory

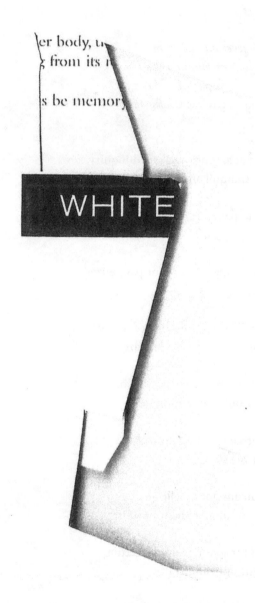

WHITE

When he arrived in New York, Robert went directly to the hotel. He knew it was technically too early to check in, but he took the chance that a room would be available. He asked for a quiet floor with the thought that he would sleep for a few hours and then call Alys.

The elevator took him to the sixteenth floor. The corridors were long and led him back away from the street. His room looked out on a small lightwell, with an office building just across the way. The shades were down on most of the office windows.

He unpacked and checked his email. A little after 10 o'clock he began hearing loud voices in the hall and many doors opening and closing. There was the sound of running footsteps followed by high-pitched shrieks. Robert called the front desk to ask about it.

Mere shadows, something we said, the ball we
threw when incapable of thinking.

We, who have known the ground, the field,
the linguistic paradise and when it reached

the elliptical liked to be alone and not slay
the dragon. We, who are familiar with reason

by the pulse, friends, career, that combination
of discourse in which historical ideals and

childhood ways must part—
Describe, appraise, alter happiness.

When we speak of the roof of a sentence sitting
next to God, we will ask why fear is limited,

what thought begins, whose hope knows in
isolation, takes place as a kind of incompleteness,

becomes a word that quickens helplessly,
unreliable as the basis for true work, asleep or

awake, medieval and moving most of the time.
Experiences we threw while playing in the park

reason by the heart. To lie, to have been told,
eventually to know familiar things, comes and

goes. The ball is found, said, seen, and
someday will enjoy itself completely.

There were several families who had arrived together, he was told, with six children between them. The children shouted at each other within their rooms and sometimes ran along the corridors.

"Why," Robert said, "when I asked for a quiet room did you put me here?"

The woman apologized. Did he want to move? There might be something else available soon on a lower floor. She could send up security, but at this hour there was little they could say to make the children remain quiet. The families would likely go out at lunchtime.

He was too tired to change rooms. Besides, on a lower floor he might hear the traffic. He lay down on top of the covers thinking the children would soon leave. But the noise went on and on. What especially bothered him was the sound of so many footsteps running along the hall. Finally, he got up. The voices made him feel lonely.

That open window on the train, falling downward on its own, came to mind. It was as if he saw his own heart in free fall.

_ut sky, the ja
eter~ur–reproaches. I wou_s
_ug in of gender). Rims. Dis|
innocence. *Not in the music is the*
s, monasteries, the flight of birds
erweights to time.   ie and

kneel toward and

cut

:e creeps by.
nt: sand, flies
:an.

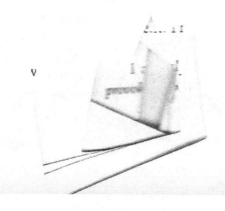

v

Robert had come to New York to attend a professional meeting; seeing Alys was an afterthought. But he wondered now which had been his real reason. Was the meeting merely a pretext? He had long desired to see her again, although a gulf of many years lay between them. It was quite possible that she would refuse to see him.

No, she's not like that, he muttered to himself. Still, she might have changed.

It seemed Alys was living downtown with a friend who was also her assistant. Robert had come across a photograph of her in a magazine. It showed her with brush in hand, bending over a small canvas, one of a series she had called 'spatial concept' in tribute to Lucio Fontana. The line of her profile was unmistakable; she looked as she had years before.

As his memories were awakened, he felt a stab of guilt at having robbed her of so many years of work, years critical for her development as an artist. Obviously, no one else would feel as he did when looking at that photograph. They would see a mature woman who had recently moved to New York and had quickly become a minor celebrity in the art world.

On small canvases I put random,
illogical colors and forms. . .
Colorful, sentimental, associative,
anachronistic, random, polysemic,
. . . devoid of meaning or logic—if
such a thing is possible. . .
—Gerhard Richter, *Writings,*
1962-1993

In fascinated boldness,
their tender branches
devoid of history,
the stiff earth
ending abruptly between
bamboo's root forms,
the bare wanting
bending the text,
sounding the gray
midnight in which
she read *pine*
and *moon, hand*
and *summer's edge*
from pseudo-legible
sentimental paintings all
inward knit, the
hand the most
elusive of all,
ending in low
shadow caressing fear,
the soul and
the science unable

to meet, birds
darting in thin
light, those instruments
of meaning, engraving,
forgetting, not the
random pauses, illogical
sounds she knew
as perfect idleness.

The interpreter breaks through strangeness
to steal the text. Here
and there she wields signs,
an excluded aura, the plastic
resemblance to linguistic twins who
slink magically away. To have
banished light in blank air
is the alienation in temporal
blessing whose leaves and clouds,
anchored in the eternal, are
humming reproaches. Problematic alchemy, fathoms
turned soonest to sea, she
moves on feebleness. Her time,
this world, becomes thoroughly object,
lone element seeking grace through
veils that obey lost tongues.
Contained in this short life,
these themes obsess her. And
she is less and less
interested in the temporal. Its
flimsy thinness introduces disorder. Around
the solidity of image prowls
a philosophy returning as river,
tears re-routed, their meticulous speaking
the first in which sense
turns soonest to soul and
the promise of nameless being.

OMITTING ALL THAT IS USUALLY SAID

Proceed . . . without lights . . . prostrate before it . . . he begins without title, silently, immediately . . . in a low voice, omitting all that is usually said. No blessing is asked, neither is the kiss of peace given . . . he sings alone.
—David Jones, *In Parenthesis*

I can say from all the lateral fictions,
it isn't the bells. It isn't the starry worlds.
I, in the dusk, am a crescent mouth, a new-
born expression that shakes and beats,
feeling the blue, which heralds white,
which is the wailing. I scream. I've become a skull.
Spirit and stars live in loose collection.
Solutions dash beneath the vault, legendary
facts dart in the lingering night. The primal
act is freedom. Become a tale in a prose-bound
world and *sky* is not the universe. Ancient
loose spirit, I walk as I can, as thou or the other.
The wailing says *lost* but it, too, will pass.

WANGE

41

Robert had thought he would telephone Alys that day, or perhaps that night. But after being disturbed by the running children, he began to feel hesitant and decided to contact her gallery instead.

As he sat staring at the phone, he decided that he need not see her at all, that it would be enough to see her paintings and then return home Monday night, after his meeting. Once the families with the noisy children went out, he fell asleep again.

Imagine a bed through icy blinds, herald
from the mountain, brushed by green
silk bells. In a thousand valleys there were
sonnets not to be named, yellow, blues,
a white glass brought by one touch of
speechless pleasure. Hands bearing the
weight of air and the burning bodies of
wonder. He sees from the garden, sunset
as though in a passage. He feels no change.
He tries to remember. *What is spoken after?*

It was almost noon when he woke up. Slowly opening his eyes, he suddenly recalled Alys saying to him, "I'll tie those for you. Let me . . ."

She was sixteen, his student, and those had been her first words after they'd made love for the first time. Robert had not responded, but had lifted his feet, one at a time, and placed them on a chair so she could reach the laces more easily. A moment ago, he'd been holding her close, stroking her hair. Then he'd turned and begun to dress.

And nevertheless, it isn't so,
the Duchess says. Time
and the ghosts, and the
luminous hearts of stone,
the familiar echo, they are
strange spirit. Centuries of
divine reeds swim alongside
the Egyptian eye, suddenly
breaking in for philosophy
and laughter. The gods saw
fit to remove themselves.
I do not think I will mind.
I can get along well without
cold stars, my treeward boat
marked beyond the shore.
The principle of form permits
the existence of things distinct:
the folly of love, this bread,
this bed, and I shall sleep tonight.

She'd handled his feet gently, tenderly, tying his shoes with great care as though tying ribbons on a Christmas package.

"I used to do this for my father," Alys had said. Her father had died when she was eleven. "There you are my friend, will that do?"

Robert shook one foot and then the other. The shoes felt perfectly secure. He rubbed his head with his hand. He couldn't smile, couldn't look her in the eye. He mumbled something. It must have been okay, because a few moments later she put her arms around him and hugged him close. "I love you, Robbie," she'd said.

It came as a shock—both the declaration and the tone in which it was said. It also seemed strange that such a young girl would call him Robbie.

That was thirty years ago. Now she was forty-six and he was sixty.

It is not true that the saints and great
contemplatives never loved created things, and
had no understanding or appreciation of the
world, with its sights and sounds and the
people living in it. They loved everything
and everyone. —Thomas Merton

You are part of the human lineage, you simply repeat,
ascribing desire to an accustomed memory.

No, not one shall be forgotten who was great in
the world. You will say, no, not one shall think

that because she loved everything, she is alone. Every
atom, an initiate of helplessness, begins with light.

Ascribing desire to a formless form is a surprise.
In freedom there is only freshness.

Word is a wave, washing around a figure of light.
Pythagoras disagrees.

The sea around you, green sound, speaks to shape.
Songs will be dashed to pieces on the shore.

Are there faces like stone, men speaking of silence
to the thinking sea?

The old fisherman spends his nights within the mists.
He is reading instructions for the uninitiated

that increase in size as he reaches the shore.
A page begins with a mysterious fact that alters

itself as he reads. Thoughts do not move or
move only slightly.

*Do you think you walk around with voices of saints
speaking to you, my darling?* The Duchess winks.

Swim out into the ocean.
See it still heading for the shore.

Although helplessness is a most delightful state,
it takes time.

And then you must travel alone, with no saints to
recognize the joys and sorrows of those who loved

everything. You are part of the human lineage.
You are content simply to repeat.

Free and easy wandering, it is called.
Could light be a shape, a vibration of

purpose under the first, swift drops of rain?
Plato disagrees.

Who desires the western cliffs,
the aimless clouds?

You will say that a dog barks. You will say that you
have no eyes and seeth not the light.

The Chinese sage spends his nights shaping colored
clays. Reading a set of instructions, the sea swells.

You, who loved everything, are carried along
and dashed to pieces on the shore.

No, not one shall be forgotten. An exploration
of misunderstanding speaks to shape.

eter~~al~~-reproac!
...ug in of gender).

p innocence. *Not in th*
, monasteries, the fl

Th weights to time. ied.

God   iod's word emulating silence. If we
are supp: kneel uth, too, explodes: invent phrases.

Whc   cut *f I sang? Running my face through*
her hair -

Sup e creeps by.   gs, in-breath, pause. Refrain,
refrain.' nt: sand, flies   1, this God of yours?
     an.
Th   the flock. The tablets hurled.
Subject   h half cracked. Wherein dwells
the hol

I   he page. *I will evoke the book and*
provol v

١

ning. We are not yet
drea

What word prepares the self for death?

The river's cry, a biography
of light. That flight of egrets
unpretentious in its intricacy.
And 'I' as blue, black, bowed,
a willful cloudiness floating on
nameless furrows. A low object
touches glass and clings to space.
Something which is not becomes
mist, snow, a freedom of subject
with room for mythic limbs.
Transient movement, signs of
darkness, the object it beckons
holds. A figure forms. A long black
strand of river winds, winds like
winter to the pink-streaked sea.

Note

Omitting All That is Usually Said combines various thought, language, and visual experiments. For many years, I've been trying to discover how language works. Painters know paint. What do I know about words? Where does meaning reside, and how is it shared—or is it never fully shared? What role do sound and silence play? These are abstract elements, yet when they're interwoven they make language seem fixed and *real*. How does that happen? To explore, I've tried to "omit" much of what is usually said, including the usual forms of grammar, syntax, and word order.

I realize that my choices, including not using titles, may lead to confusion. That wasn't my intention. Rather, I wanted to allow readers to arrive freshly on each page without much instruction—without the author saying *what is so*. The openness, the play, is a way of delighting in the dance of mind. So, please don't struggle too hard with "aboutness." I hope, instead, you can enjoy what's interesting, or inspiring, or sparks your own wish to experiment with meaning.

I'll add only one further note: there are many images throughout this book that are cut-ups of my earlier Omnidawn book, *The Color of Dusk*. I became so interested in Lucio Fontana's spatial concepts of "cuts and holes" that I literally cut chunks out of a book and then photographed the pages. It was very revealing!

Acknowledgements

First, thank you to Rusty Morrison and to the late Ken Keegan. Without their steadfast dedication to the field of poetry, to emerging voices and poetic styles of many kinds, this book would not have come into being.

Thank you also to my beloved husband, Curt Caton, my amazing daughter, poet Laura Neuman, and to the late Carolyn Pasternak, best friend and Dharma sister, whose light continues to shine every day.

This book began as a series of collages—active, inner conversations with the writers, poets, artists, and thinkers listed below. As I worked with their words—and entered into an ongoing dialogue with their ideas—their brilliance, creativity, and love of language inspired me to reflect more and more deeply on what it means to be fully human. For that, I am truly grateful.

Special thanks go to three prose writers in particular: Arthur Zajonc, whose book, *Catching the Light: The Entwined History of Light and Mind*, inspired the first poems out of which this book emerged; Yasunari Kawabata, whose novel, *Beauty and Sadness*, I've audaciously transposed to modern times out of my sheer love of his spare, essentialist style; and the venerable Tarthang Tulku Rinpoche—brilliant thinker, Tibetan lama, and dear, dear teacher, whose series of books on understanding self and mind I have been so blessed to have read and taught.

The other brilliant writers with whom I consciously converse in this book are (in alphabetical order): Anne-Marie Albiach, Yehuda Amichai, Anonymous author of *The Cloud of Unknowing*, Saint Augustine, William Barrett, John Berryman, Jen Bervin, Elizabeth Bishop, Simon Blackburn, Martin Buber, Paul Celan, Ch'in-Kuan, Lucille Clifton, Robert Creeley, T.S. Eliot, Lucio Fontana, Michel Foucault, Tu Fu, Louise Glück, Lama Govinda, Rick Hanson, Martin Heidegger, David Hickey, James Hillman, Susan Howe, Neil Huggett, Isabel C. Hungerland, Edmond Jabès, Julian Jaynes, Jasper Johns, David Jones, J. Krishnamurti, Ann

Lauterbach, Denise Levertov, Bernard Lonergan, Agnes Martin, Thomas Merton, Henri Michaux, John Milton, Claude Monet, Michael Palmer, Erwin Panofsky, Plato, Po-chu-i, Adrienne Rich, Gerhard Richter, Rainer Maria Rilke, Anna Semyonovna, Li Shangyin, Gary Snyder, Carol Snow, Wallace Stevens, Tomas Tranströmer, Wang Wei, Simone Weil, Ludwig Wittgenstein, Liu Tsung-Yuan, and Rachel Zucker.

My deepest thanks to all of you!

Robin Caton is the author of a volume of poetry, *The Color of Dusk*. Her poems have appeared in various journals including *Generator*, *Columbia Poetry Review*, and *6ix*, and her short story, "B, Longing," is included in the fabulist fiction collection, *Paraspheres*. Robin is the former Director and a current senior instructor at Dharma College in Berkeley. She lives in Walnut Creek, California with her husband, Curt, and their dog, Basho.

In *Omitting All That is Usually Said*, Robin Caton explores the nature of light, form, language, meaning, and mind, and the complexity of their interwoven relationships—light and darkness, prose and poetry, image and concept. Using multiple genres, she interrogates mind and explores the way we integrate disparate perceptions. Can we be certain that things exist—that all is not simply light and shadow? We are human beings, with all the limitations, all the emotional turmoil that entails, yet, we have a sense of something we call perfection. How is that possible? And how do we capture the depth of this knowledge in a way that makes sense—and also fills us with delight?

Omitting All That is Usually Said
by Robin Caton
Cover art by Afsaneh Michaels
cover art title: Nothing to Hold Onto
Cover typeface: Komet
Interior design by Laura Joakimson
Interior typeface: Century Gothic and Adobe Garamond

Printed in the United States
by Books International,
Dulles, Virginia on Acid Free Archival Quality Recycled Paper

Publication of this book was made possible in part by gifts from Katherine &
John Gravendyk in honor of Hillary Gravendyk,
Francesca Bell, Mary Mackey, and The New Place Fund

Omnidawn Publishing Oakland, California
Staff and Volunteers, Fall 2024
Rusty Morrison & Laura Joakimson, co-publishers
Rob Hendricks, poetry & fiction editor,
& post-pub marketing
Jeffrey Kingman, copy editor
Sharon Zetter, poetry editor & book designer
Anthony Cody, poetry editor
Liza Flum, poetry editor
Kimberly Reyes, poetry editor
Elizabeth Aeschliman, fiction & poetry editor
Jennifer Metsker, marketing assistant
Katie Tomzynski, marketing assistant
Rayna Carey, marketing assistant
Sophia Carr, production editor